Livingston

by Iain Gray

WRITING *to* REMEMBER

Lang**Syne**

PUBLISHING

WRITING *to* REMEMBER

79 Main Street, Newtongrange,
Midlothian EH22 4NA
Tel: 0131 344 0414
E-mail: info@lang-syne.co.uk
www.langsyneshop.co.uk

Design by Dorothy Meikle
Printed by Blissetts
© Lang Syne Publishers Ltd 2024

All rights reserved. No part of this publication may be reproduced, stored or introduced into a retrieval system, or transmitted in any form or by any means (electronic, mechanical, photocopying, recording or otherwise) without the prior written permission of Lang Syne Publishers Ltd.

ISBN 978-1-85217-772-0

Livingston

MOTTOES include:
If I can *(Livingston)*
Hill of Fire *(Clan MacLea)*

CRESTS include:
A demi-savage, wreathed on the head and body, holding a club on the right shoulder and a serpent in the left hand *(Livingston)*

A demi-man holding the staff of St Moluag in his right hand and a cross crosslet fitchée in his left *(Clan MacLea)*

TERRITORIES include:
West Lothian, Falkirk, Isle of Lismore

NAME variations include:
Livingstone
Livington
MacLea
Mac-an-Leigh
MacDunsleibh
MacDuinnsleibhe

Chapter one:

The origins of the clan system

by Rennie McOwan

The original Scottish clans of the Highlands and the great families of the Lowlands and Borders were gatherings of families, relatives, allies and neighbours for mutual protection against rivals or invaders.

Scotland experienced invasion from the Vikings, the Romans and English armies from the south. The Norman invasion of what is now England also had an influence on land-holding in Scotland. Some of these invaders stayed on and in time became 'Scottish'.

The word clan derives from the Gaelic language term 'clann', meaning children, and it was first used many centuries ago as communities were formed around tribal lands in glens and mountain fastnesses.

The format of clans changed over the centuries, but at its best the chief and his family held theland on behalf of all, like trustees, and the ordinary clansmen and women believed they had a blood relationship with the founder of their clan.

There were two way duties and obligations. An inadequate chief could be deposed and replaced by someone of greater ability.

Clan people had an immense pride in race. Their relationship with the chief was like adult children to a father and they had a real dignity.

The concept of clanship is very old and a more feudal notion of authority gradually crept in.

Pictland, for instance, was divided into seven principalities ruled by feudal leaders who were the strongest and most charismatic leaders of their particular groups.

By the sixth century the 'British' kingdoms of Strathclyde, Lothian and Celtic Dalriada (Argyll) had emerged and Scotland, as one nation, began to take shape in the time of King Kenneth MacAlpin.

Some chiefs claimed descent from ancient kings which may not have been accurate in every case.

By the twelfth and thirteenth centuries the clans and families were more strongly brought under the central control of Scottish monarchs.

Lands were awarded and administered more and more under royal favour, yet the power of the area clan chiefs was still very great.

The long wars to ensure Scotland's

independence against the expansionist ideas of English monarchs extended the influence of some clans and reduced the lands of others.

Those who supported Scotland's greatest king, Robert the Bruce, were awarded the territories of the families who had opposed his claim to the Scottish throne.

In the Scottish Borders country – the notorious Debatable Lands – the great families built up a ferocious reputation for providing warlike men accustomed to raiding into England and occasionally fighting one another.

Chiefs had the power to dispense justice and to confiscate lands and clan warfare produced a society where martial virtues – courage, hardiness, tenacity – were greatly admired.

Gradually the relationship between the clans and the Crown became strained as Scottish monarchs became more orientated to life in the Lowlands and, on occasion, towards England.

The Highland clans spoke a different language, Gaelic, whereas the language of Lowland Scotland and the court was Scots and in more modern times, English.

Highlanders dressed differently, had different

customs, and their wild mountain land sometimes seemed almost foreign to people living in the Lowlands.

It must be emphasised that Gaelic culture was very rich and story-telling, poetry, piping, the clarsach (harp) and other music all flourished and were greatly respected.

Highland culture was different from other parts of Scotland but it was not inferior or less sophisticated.

Central Government, whether in London or Edinburgh, sometimes saw the Gaelic clans as a challenge to their authority and some sent expeditions into the Highlands and west to crush the power of the Lords of the Isles.

Nevertheless, when the eighteenth century Jacobite Risings came along the cause of the Stuarts was mainly supported by Highland clans.

The word Jacobite comes from the Latin for James – Jacobus. The Jacobites wanted to restore the exiled Stuarts to the throne of Britain.

The monarchies of Scotland and England became one in 1603 when King James VI of Scotland (1st of England) gained the English throne after Queen Elizabeth died.

The Union of Parliaments of Scotland and England, the Treaty of Union, took place in 1707.

Some Highland clans, of course, and Lowland families opposed the Jacobites and supported the incoming Hanoverians.

After the Jacobite cause finally went down at Culloden in 1746 a kind of ethnic cleansing took place. The power of the chiefs was curtailed. Tartan and the pipes were banned in law.

Many emigrated, some because they wanted to, some because they were evicted by force. In addition, many Highlanders left for the cities of the south to seek work.

Many of the clan lands became home to sheep and deer shooting estates.

But the warlike traditions of the clans and the great Lowland and Border families lived on, with their descendants fighting bravely for freedom in two world wars.

Remember the men from whence you came, says the Gaelic proverb, and to that could be added the role of many heroic women.

The spirit of the clan, of having roots, whether Highland or Lowland, means much to thousands of people.

Meanwhile, many families proudly boast the heraldic device known as a Coat of Arms,.

The central motif of the Coat of Arms would originally have been what was sometimes borne on the shield of a warrior to distinguish himself from others on the battlefield.

Clan warfare produced a society where courage and tenacity were greatly admired

Chapter two:

Aristocratic roots

A locational surname 'Livingston' and its popular spelling variant 'Livingstone' feature prominently in the pages of the vibrant drama that is Scotland's history.

The name is intriguing in that it derives from the ancient Anglo-Saxon 'Leving', while there are two possible explanations as to how such a family came to be in what is now modern day West Lothian, on Scotland's east coast, and subsequently gave their name – in the form of 'Livingston' – to the present day village and town.

One legend relating to their origins is that an Anglo-Saxon by the name of 'Leving' was granted the lands in West Lothian during the reign from 1124 to 1153 of King David I, the youngest of the three sons of King Malcolm III.

David had spent time in captivity in England but, despite this, had become enamoured with some customs and manners.

Accordingly, he invited Anglo-Norman families to settle in Scotland – granting them lands in the full knowledge that to protect and retain them they would serve his own interests by helping to uphold the authority of the crown through quelling 'rebellious' native Scots.

While it is known that he did indeed invite Anglo-Normans to settle, he may well have also invited Anglo-Saxons such as the Levings also to migrate from south of the border.

But another possibility is that the Levings may have been among those members of the Anglo-Saxon aristocracy who were forced to quit their original territory in Northumbria in the late eleventh century.

This was in the aftermath of a vicious purge launched against them and fellow aristocratic families and Danish settlers by William the Conqueror, victor of the battle of Hastings in 1066.

Following his defeat of King Harold II, the last Anglo-Saxon king, William was declared king and the complete subjugation of his subjects followed, with those Normans who had fought on his behalf rewarded with lands.

But trouble brewed for William in the north of his new realm, where Anglo-Danish rebellions had been stirred by Edgar Atheling, claimant to what had been the kingdom of Wessex.

In what is known as The Harrying of the North, William's response was brutal – laying waste from 1069 to 1070 to the northern shires, including the city of York and replacing native aristocracy – such as those, it is reasonable to suggest, who would come to bear the Livingston name in Scotland – with Normans deemed more loyal.

In 1071, King Malcolm III of Scotland married Margaret, a sister of the Saxon Edgar Atheling and therefore had an affinity with the dispossessed northerners – welcoming them to settle in his realm.

But when, or by whatever means, the Livingstons first arrived in Scotland, what is known with certainty is that in 1296, in the now redundant form 'Levingestoune', Sir Archibald de (of) Levingestoune appears as a signatory to an infamous document.

In July of that year, the Scots rose in revolt against the imperialist designs of England's King Edward I.

But, known as 'the Hammer of the Scots' following his earlier crushing of the rising led by the great freedom fighter William Wallace, he brought the entire nation under his subjugation little less than a month later, garrisoning strategic locations throughout the nation and demanding the signing of a humiliating treaty of fealty.

Reluctantly signed at Berwick by 1,500 Scottish earls, bishops and burgesses, the parchment is known as the *Ragman Roll* because of the profusion of ribbons that dangle from the seals of the signatories – among whom was Sir Archibald de Levingestoune.

The fact that he is among the signatories indicates that he was considered influential enough in Scottish affairs to be required to do so.

This status was destined to reach impressive new heights over the succeeding centuries as the family acquired glittering honours and distinction including the Barony and then the earldoms of Callendar, Linlithgow and Newburgh and the viscountships of Kilsyth, Kinnaird and Teviot.

While the Livingstons were meanwhile establishing themselves in the Lowlands, a clan known as 'the Highland Livingstons' had been settled for a number of centuries before in the western district of Lorn, Argyll.

Known as Clan Mac-an-Leigh, or MacLea and with their seat at Bachuil, on the Isle of Lismore, there are a number of theories regarding their origin.

But the consensus is that they descend from the Royal Family of Ulster, while Gaelic renderings of their name include *Mac-an-Leigh*, *MacDunsleibh* and *MacDuinnsleibhe*.

Although their proud history and traditions are wholly separate from those of the Livingstons, they are believed to have adopted the Livingston/Livingstone surname at some stage during the reign from 1625 to 1649 of King Charles I when Sir William Livingston of Skirling, Peeblesshire, was granted a lease on Achanduin Castle, on Lismore.

The MacLea chief, meanwhile, is recognised today by the Lord Lyon King of Arms of Scotland as the Hereditary Keeper of the Pastoral Staff of St Moluag – the Irish missionary who was born about 520.

The Livingstons and Clan MacLea also have separate Coats of Arms.

The Livingston motto is 'If I can' and crest a demi-savage, wreathed on the head and body, holding a club on the right shoulder and a serpent in the left hand.

The MacLea motto, referring to the site of an ancient burial mound at Bachuil, translates from Gaelic as 'Hill of fire', while the crest features a demi-man holding the staff of St Moluag in his right hand and a cross crosslet fitchée in his left.

The clan chief, at the time of writing, is Niall Livingstone of Bachuil.

Returning to the Lowland Livingstons, James Livingston, whose father Sir Archibald had been one of the signatories to the *Ragman Roll* of 1296, was among the 12,000 Scots who fought under the overall command of King David II at the battle of Neville's Cross, about half a mile west of Durham, in October of 1346.

Also known as the battle of Durham, and fought under the terms of Scotland's Auld Alliance with France that required David to fulfil an obligation to invade England while it was at war with France during the Hundred Years' War, the 7,000-strong English army was commanded by Ralph Neville, Lord Neville.

The Scots were soundly defeated, with an estimated 3,000, including four earls and more than 50 barons, killed.

To add to Scotland's woes, their king was among those captured and not released until eleven years after the battle on payment of a ransom worth a staggering £62m in today's terms.

James Livingston was among the Scottish nobles who were also captured, but released for ransom shortly afterwards and, once back in his homeland, acted as one of the commissioners for his king's release – and subsequently rewarded by the monarch with the grant of the Barony of Callendar, in the present day local authority area of Falkirk.

Sited in Callendar Park, Callendar House, dating back to the fourteenth century but extensively redesigned and extended in the nineteenth, this seat of James Livingston and his descendants for a time is now an A listed building in the care of Falkirk Community Trust.

In common with many other iconic Scottish locations, it has also featured as a location for the popular historical drama series *Outlander*.

Chapter three:

Fame and infamy

It was not only fame that attached itself to the Livingston name as its bearers accrued lands and titles but also infamy – particularly in the case of Sir Alexander Livingston of Callendar.

Keeper of Stirling Castle for a period during the minority of King James II and Justiciar of Scotland, he conspired with William Crichton, the Lord Chancellor, in the infamous affair known as the 'Black Dinner.'

On the night of November 24, 1440, the boy-king James and a glittering retinue of nobles and courtiers had gathered in the banqueting hall of Edinburgh Castle for a feast in honour of the young Earl of Douglas.

But it was no ordinary feast, because treachery hung heavy in the air – with the festivities ending in the slaughter of the earl and his younger brother.

James had been aged only six when, in 1437, he was enthroned as King of Scots following the assassination of his father James I in a conspiracy orchestrated by some of his nobles.

Whoever controlled the young king controlled the country, and James became the subject of a virtual tug-of-war between powerful and ambitious magnates.

At the forefront of this struggle were Sir Alexander Livingston and Sir William Crichton, but they agreed to temporarily suspend their rivalry when they became aware of a threat to their schemes.

This came in the form of William, Earl of Douglas, who had succeeded to the title following the death of his father in 1437.

As head of the branch of the Douglas family known as the Black Douglases, the 17-year-old earl owned vast tracts of land in the southwest while another branch, the Red Douglases, held sway over territories in the northeast.

Ignoring the advice of wiser heads, the earl accepted a flattering invitation from the king, at the behest of the scheming Livingston and Crichton, to come to Edinburgh to 'help in advising for the good of the realm.'

A magnificent feast had been laid out in the castle's banqueting hall and the mood was jocular as the earl, flattered by the attention he was receiving, chatted easily with the young king.

But the mood abruptly turned sour when Crichton rose from his place at table and accused the House of Douglas of disloyalty to the Crown.

A servant then entered the hall carrying a gruesome splendour.

A fearsome silence descended on the hall, as all present were aware that the black bull's head, known as the 'black cap', was an ancient symbol of doom and signified death.

The doom it heralded was that of the earl and his brother, who were quickly bound and seized by armed men.

The king, shocked at the treacherous treatment of his guests, pleaded for mercy to be shown to the brothers – only to be coldly informed by Livingston and Crichton: 'Either you or they must die, for the kingdom of Scotland cannot hold both a Stuart and a Douglas.'

A summary trial was held and sentence passed on the brothers.

Dragged from the hall, they were led out to the courtyard, where an execution block had already been set up, and beheaded one after another.

In the tortuous power struggles of the time when loyalties constantly fluctuated, Sir Alexander

Livingston later allied himself with the Douglases against Crichton.

He died in 1451, while one of his descendants, also named Alexander, was Alexander Livingston, 5th Lord Livingston of Callendar, one of the eight 'Lord Keepers' of Mary Queen of Scots during her infancy.

He accompanied her to France in 1548 following her betrothal to the young French Dauphin Francis II, remaining there until his death in 1553.

Through his second marriage to Lady Agnes Douglas, daughter of John Douglas, 2nd Earl of Morton, he was the father of Mary Livingston, born in about 1541 and who, along with Mary Beaton, Mary Fleming and Mary Seaton was one of the young queen's ladies-in-waiting more famously known as 'The Four Marys'.

In attendance to the queen throughout her time at the French court and later married to John Sempill of Bruntschiells and Beltrees, she is portrayed in the 2018 film Mary Queen of Scots by the actress Liah O'Prey.

Honours and titles meanwhile continued to accrue to the Livingstons over the succeeding centuries as they suffered both glorious fortune and tragic misfortune including the forfeiture of some titles.

In their original heartland of West Lothian, however, their name remains on the landscape in the form of the 'New Town' of Livingston, west of Edinburgh. Built in 1962 as one of a number of Scottish 'New Towns' and further developed in the 1980s, it still retains part of the original village, now known as Livingston Village.

One of the most famous bearers of the name, in the popular spelling variant 'Livingstone', was the Scottish Christian missionary, explorer and physician David Livingstone who, because of his resilience in the face of adversity and dogged determination, remains an inspiration for many today.

Africa, where his legacy was established, was not only many thousands of miles from the land of his birth, but many of its vast regions and inhabitants were unknown to the West.

Livingstone was destined to change that.

Born in 1813 in the mill town of Blantyre, South Lanarkshire, the second of seven children, he was raised in a strict Christian household, with his father – a door-to-door tea salesman and a Church of Scotland Sunday School teacher – and mother devoted to the faith and its moral codes.

In common with his parents, Livingstone

also had an inquiring mind and a passion for learning and, when not toiling twelve hours a day from the age of ten in a cotton mill, found time to study.

By the time he was aged 23 – having left the Church of Scotland along with his father in favour of the Congregational Church – he was able to study theology and Greek at Anderson's College, Glasgow, now today's centre of academic excellence the University of Strathclyde, while two years later he studied medicine in London and qualified as a physician.

Also having undertaken missionary training under the London Missionary Society (LMS), he embarked on the first of what would be three separate pioneering exploratory and missionary expeditions to what was known then as the Dark Continent.

Setting up a mission in Mabosta, in Botswana, in 1845, he later journeyed up the Zambesi River, becoming the first European to see the waterfall known as Mosi-o-Tunya, 'the smoke that thunders', and named it the Victoria Falls in honour of Queen Victoria.

Mapping most of the course of the mighty Zambesi and also becoming the first European to cross south-central Africa, he immediately became famous and hailed as the explorer who 'opened up' Africa – spreading the Christian message as he did so.

Returning for a time to Britain, where he became a persuasive advocate for action against the African slave trade as then carried out by the Portuguese, he also argued it could be replaced through other more humane commercial enterprises, all rallied under the banner of Christianity.

"Christianity, Commerce and Civilisation" became his motto and, fittingly, this is inscribed today on his statue at the Victoria Falls.

His second expedition to the continent, from March 1858 to the middle of 1864, the Second Zambezi Expedition, saw him brave fever and other severe handicaps with the famous quotation: "I am prepared to go anywhere, provided it be forward."

His final mission to Africa was in 1866 in a brave but nonetheless unsuccessful attempt to locate the source of the Nile, reaching Lake Malawi in August of that year but being struck by a serious of increasingly debilitating illnesses.

Still attempting to battle on with the aid of a band of faithful native retainers, he had lost all contact with the outside world for more than five years.

This was until he was located in the town

of Ujiji, on the shores of Lake Tanganyika, on November 10, 1871, by the *New York Herald* journalist Henry Morton Stanley – who is reputed to have greeted the emaciated figure that was the famous explorer with the words: "Dr Livingstone, I presume?"

Despite Stanley's plea to Livingstone to return home, he adamantly refused and, stricken by malaria and other afflictions he died on May 1, 1873, aged 60, at Ilala, in present day Zambia.

His heart was buried under a tree near the spot where he died, and native bearers transported his remains to the coast for return to Britain and subsequent internment in Westminster Abbey.

In addition to numerous honours and accolades that include the gold medal of the Royal Geographical Society and his statue at the Victoria Falls, he is also honoured through a number of other memorials and institutions that include the splendid David Livingstone Centre in his birth place of Blantyre.

Operated by the David Livingstone Trust and set in parkland, its museum displays an impressive explorer and missionary's life and times.

Chapter four:

On the world stage

From music and the stage to sport, enterprise and science, bearers of the Livingston and Livingstone names have gained international fame and acclaim.

Born in Pittsburgh, Pennsylvania in 1915, Jacob Harold Levison was the award-winning American songwriter better known as **Jay Livingston**.

With Livingston writing the music and his partner Ray Evans the lyrics, the pair won three Academy Awards for Best Original Song featured in film.

These were for the 1948 *Buttons and Bows*, written for *Paleface*, the 1950 *Mona Lisa* for *Captain Carey, U.S.A.* and, from 1956, *Que Sera, Sera (Whatever Will Be, Will Be)* for *The Man Who Knew Too Much*.

Having also written the Christmas favourite *Silver Bells* and the Johnny Mathis hit *All TheTime* and an inductee of the Songwriters Hall of Fame, he died in 2001.

His younger brother **Alan Livingston**, born Alan Wendell Levison in 1917, was the writer and producer best known for his work with Capitol Records and the NBC television network.

Joining Capital Records at the end of the Second World War, he wrote a series of story-telling records for children including *Bozo the Clown* and the 1951 Mel Blane hit *I Tawt I Taw a Puddy Tat* for the Tweety Pie character.

Through the Capitol Records subsidiary Electrical and Media Industries (EMI), he was responsible for the release in the United States of the Beatles' 1963 hit *I Want to Hold Your Hand*, while also later signing artists and bands including Frank Sinatra, Steve Miller and the Beach Boys.

With NBC for a time as vice-president in charge of programming, he also oversaw the development and launch of the highly popular Western *Bonanza*.

He died in 2009, while in contemporary times **Bob Livingston** is the American singer, songwriter and guitarist born in 1948 in San Antonio, Texas.

A founding member in the early 1970s of The Lost Gonzo Band and regarded as a key figure in the genres 'progressive country' and 'outlaw country', his best-selling solo albums include the 2011 *Gypsy*

Alibi, while he is an inductee of the Texas Music Legends Hall of Fame.

On the stage, **Barry Livingston** is the American television and film actor best known for his role from 1963 to 1972 of Ernie Douglas in the popular series *My Three Sons*.

Born in Los Angeles in 1953 and as a child actor appearing in the 1958 Paul Newman film *Rally 'Round the Flag, Boys!* he is the younger brother of the actor **Bernard Livingston**, born in 1950 and who also appeared in *My Three Sons*, in the role of Chip Douglas.

Also on American shores, **Ron Livingston** is the actor known for his big screen roles in films including the 1996 *Swingers*, the 1999 *Office Space* and, from 2013, *The Conjuring*.

Born in 1967 in Cedar Rapids, Iowa, his television credits include the mini-series *Band of Brothers*, *Loudermilk* and *Boardwalk Empire*.

On Australian shores, **Paul Livingston** is the comedian and playwright also known as **Flacco**.

Born in Sydney in 1956 and having appeared in television shows including *Good News Week*, *The Sideshow* and *Flacco Special*, as a playwright he wrote the acclaimed 2001 *Emma's Nose*, while he has also appeared at festivals including the annual Edinburgh Festival.

Bearers of the Livingston/Livingstone names have also excelled in the highly competitive world of sport.

On the football pitch, **Dugald Livingstone** was the Scottish player and manager better known as 'Dug', 'Doug' or *'Duggie' Livingstone*.

Born in 1898 in Alexandria, West Dunbartonshire, teams he played for before embarking on a career in management with not only clubs but international teams, include Aberdeen, Celtic, Everton and Tranmere Rovers.

Manager of the Republic of Ireland team from 1951 to 1953 he then managed Belgium – notably guiding them to qualify for the 1954 World Cup, where they achieved a 4-4 draw with England in the group stages.

Later managing Newcastle, Fulham and Chesterfield, he died in 1981.

Combining enterprise with football, **Ian Livingstone** is the Scottish businessman who served from 1973 to 1987 as chairman of Motherwell Football Club.

Born in 1938 in Hamilton, South Lanarkshire

and a senior partner with a Motherwell-based firm of solicitors, he has been chairman of his family investment and development company, while from 1991 to 2000 he served as chairman of Lanarkshire Development Agency.

Also a former chairman of Lanarkshire Health Board, other positions he has held include governor and chairman of the David Livingstone Memorial Trust, while in 1998 he was appointed CBE for services to the community and health in Lanarkshire.

Also combining business with a passion for football, Ian Livingston, more formally known as **Baron Livingston of Parkhead**, was born in Glasgow in 1964, the fourth generation son of Polish-Lithuanian Jews who settled in Scotland.

Having trained as an accountant, he was appointed the first chief accountant of *The Independent* newspaper, later joining the Dixon Group where he was instrumental in the creation of PC World and the broadband provider Freeserve.

Later chief executive of BT Group, as a Celtic fan he joined the club as a non-executive director in 2007.

Created a life peer in 2013 as Baron

Livingston of Parkhead – 'Parkhead' the name of Celtic's ground in the east end of Glasgow – he has served as a Conservative member in the House of Lords, and previously as the government's Minister of State for Trade and Investment.

In the world of science, **Milton Livingston** was the pioneering American physicist who, along with Ernest Lawrence, was co-inventor of the particle accelerator the cyclotron.

Serving during the Second World War in the operations research group at the Office of Naval Research and later chairman of the Accelerator Project at Brookhaven National Laboratory, Long Island, he was also the author of a number of papers on nuclear physics and the cyclotron.

The recipient of honours and awards including the Enrico Fermi Award from the United States Department of Energy, he died in 1986.

Taking to the skies, **John H. Livingston** was the American aviator and air racer who, during the early twentieth century, won a number of prestigious races in aircraft including his specially modified Monocoupe 110 Special.

Born in 1897 in Cedar Falls, Iowa, he worked for a time with the Iowa Airplane Company, while he won his first race in 1928, the Transcontinental Air Derby, piloting a Waco 10T from New York to Los Angeles.

An inductee of the Iowa Aviation Hall of Fame, he died in 1974, while he is considered to be the inspiration for the author and pilot Richard Bach's 1970 novel *Jonathan Livingston Seagull* – adapted for the film of the name in 1973.

In the world of contemporary British politics, Kenneth Robert Livingstone is the former Labour Party member and London Mayor better known as **Ken Livingstone**.

Born in Lambeth, South London in 1945 and also known as 'Red Ken' because of his hard-left views, he served as an Independent as London Mayor from 2000 until 2004 and, re-elected as a Labour member, from 2004 until 2008 when he was succeeded by future Conservative Prime Minister Boris Johnston.

Suspended from the Labour Party in 2016 over controversial comments regarding the Nazis and Zionism, he resigned from the party two years later.

In the realms of fantasy, **Ian Livingstone**, born in 1949, is the English author and entrepreneur who, along with Steve Jackson, is co-founder of the role-playing gamebooks' series *Fighting Fantasy*.

Also co-founder, in 1975, of Games Workshop – which obtained the exclusive rights in Europe to top-selling game *Dungeons and Dragons* – and winner of the 2002 BAFTA Interactive Special Award for Outstanding Contribution to the Industry, he was appointed CBE in 2013 for services to the computer gaming industry.